BASEBALL LEGENDS

Hank Aaron
Grover Cleveland Alexander
Ernie Banks
Johnny Bench
Yogi Berra
Roy Campanella
Roberto Clemente
Ty Cobb
Dizzy Dean
Joe DiMaggio
Bob Feller
Jimmie Foxx
Lou Gehrig
Bob Gibson
Rogers Hornsby
Walter Johnson
Sandy Koufax
Mickey Mantle
Christy Mathewson
Willie Mays
Stan Musial
Satchel Paige
Brooks Robinson
Frank Robinson
Jackie Robinson
Babe Ruth
Duke Snider
Warren Spahn
Willie Stargell
Honus Wagner
Ted Williams
Carl Yastrzemski
Cy Young

CHELSEA HOUSE PUBLISHERS

WALTER JOHNSON

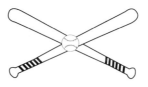

Jack Kavanagh

Introduction by
Jim Murray

Senior Consultant
Earl Weaver

CHELSEA HOUSE PUBLISHERS
New York • Philadelphia

Published by arrangement with
Chelsea House Publishers.
Newfield Publications is a federally
registered trademark of Newfield
Publications, Inc.

Produced by James Charlton Associates
New York, New York.

Designed by Hudson Studio
Ossining, New York.

Typesetting by LinoGraphics
New York, New York.

Picture research by Carolann Hawkins
Cover illustration by Dan O'Leary

Library of Congress Cataloging-in-Publication Data

Kavanagh, Jack.
    Walter Johnson / Jack Kavanagh ; introduction by Jim Murray ;
  senior consultant, Earl Weaver.
        p.   cm. — (Baseball legends)
    Includes bibliographical references and index.
    Summary: A biography of the Hall of Fame baseball player who
  was deemed the greatest pitcher of his era.
        ISBN 0-7910-1179-8. — ISBN 0-7910-1213-1 (pbk.)
    1. Johnson, Walter Perry, 1887-1946—Juvenile literature.
    2. Baseball players—United States—Biography—Juvenile
  literature. 3. Pitchers (Baseball)—United States—Biography—
  ‚Juvenile literature. [1. Johnson, Walter Perry, 1887-1946. 2.
  Baseball players.] I. Title. II. Series.
  GV865.J6K38 1991   91-518
  796.357'092—dc20   CIP
  [B]   AC

CONTENTS

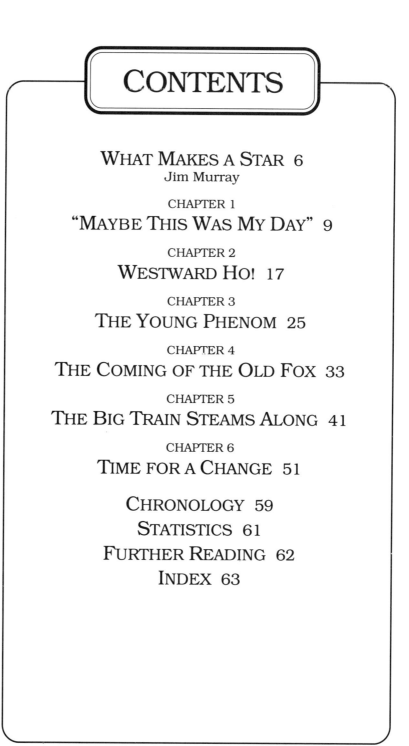

WHAT MAKES A STAR 6
Jim Murray

CHAPTER 1
"MAYBE THIS WAS MY DAY" 9

CHAPTER 2
WESTWARD HO! 17

CHAPTER 3
THE YOUNG PHENOM 25

CHAPTER 4
THE COMING OF THE OLD FOX 33

CHAPTER 5
THE BIG TRAIN STEAMS ALONG 41

CHAPTER 6
TIME FOR A CHANGE 51

CHRONOLOGY 59
STATISTICS 61
FURTHER READING 62
INDEX 63

WHAT MAKES A STAR

Jim Murray

No one has ever been able to explain to me the mysterious alchemy that makes one man a .350 hitter and another player, more or less identical in physical makeup, hard put to hit .200. You look at an Al Kaline, who played with the Detroit Tigers from 1953 to 1974. He was pale, stringy, almost poetic-looking. He always seemed to be struggling against a bad case of mononucleosis. But with a bat in his hands, he was King Kong. During his career, he hit 399 home runs, rapped out 3,007 hits, and compiled a .297 batting average.

Form isn't the reason. The first time anybody saw Roberto Clemente step into the batter's box for the Pittsburgh Pirates, the best guess was that Clemente would be back in Double A ball in a week. He had one foot in the bucket and held his bat at an awkward angle—he looked as though he couldn't hit an outside pitch. A lot of other ballplayers may have had a better-looking stance. Yet they never led the National League in hitting in four different years, the way Clemente did.

Not every ballplayer is born with the ability to hit a curveball. Nor is exceptional hand-eye coordination the key to heavy hitting. Big-league locker rooms are filled with players who have all the attributes, save one: discipline. Every baseball man can tell you a story about a pitcher who throws a ball faster than anyone has ever seen but who has no control on or *off* the field.

The Hall of Fame is full of people who transformed themselves into great ballplayers by working at the sport, by studying the game, and making sacrifices. They're overachievers—and winners. If you want to find them, just watch the World Series. Or simply read about New York Yankee great Lou Gehrig; Ted Williams, "the Splendid Splinter" of the Boston Red Sox; or the Dodgers' strikeout king Sandy Koufax.

A pitcher *should* be able to win a lot of ballgames with a 98-miles-per-hour fastball. But what about the pitcher who wins 20 games a year with a fastball so slow that you can catch it with your teeth? Bob Feller of the Cleveland Indians got into the Hall of Fame with a blazing fastball that glowed in the dark. National League star Grover Cleveland Alexander got there with a pitch that took considerably longer to reach the plate; but when it did arrive, the pitch was exactly where Alexander wanted it to be—and the last place the batter expected it to be.

There are probably more players with exceptional ability who didn't make it to the major leagues than there are who did. A number of great hitters, bored with fielding practice, had to be dropped from their team because their home-run production didn't make up for their lapses in the field. And then there are players like Brooks Robinson of the Baltimore Orioles, who made himself into a human vacuum cleaner at third base because he knew that working hard to become an expert fielder would win him a job in the big leagues.

A star is not something that flashes through the sky. That's a comet. Or a meteor. A star is something you can steer ships by. It stays in place and gives off a steady glow; it is fixed, permanent. A star works at being a star.

And that's how you tell a star in baseball. He shows up night after night and takes pride in how brightly he shines. He's Willie Mays running so hard his hat keeps falling off; Ty Cobb sliding to stretch a single into a double; Lou Gehrig, after being fooled in his first two at-bats, belting the next pitch off the light tower because he's taken the time to study the pitcher. Stars never take themselves for granted. That's why they're stars.

"MAYBE THIS WAS MY DAY"

Duringthe 1924 season, Walter Johnson won the 374th game of his big-league career. That feat made him the second-winningest pitcher in baseball history. Only the great Cy Young's 511 victories topped Johnson's total.

The Big Train—as the 200-pound, 6-foot 1-inch Johnson was sometimes called—had won his first game in 1907. Back then, he was still a ruddy-faced teenager from a Kansas farm. In 1924, however, he was a grown man with five children and the shining star of the Washington Senators' pitching staff, as he had been for the past 18 years.

During that long stretch, Johnson never notched a victory in the World Series. He had long since established himself as the American League's all-time winningest pitcher. But the Senators were not a winning ballclub. It took them their first two dozen years in the American

Some famous baseball figures pose together before the start of the 1924 World Series. From left to right are: Fred Lieb, writer and chief scorer for the series; Nick Altrock; Ty Cobb; Babe Ruth; John McGraw; Walter Johnson; George Sisler; and Christy Walsh, sportswriter and manager of Ruth.

League to beat out the other seven teams and make it into the Series. When they finally captured the American League pennant in 1924, though, Walter Johnson was ready.

If playing for the championship was a unique thrill for Johnson and the Senators, it was no big deal for their opponents. The New York Giants had been the National League champions 8 times in the last 14 years and had just won their fourth straight pennant.

They looked even stronger in 1924. Travis Jackson, a future Hall of Famer, took over the shortstop position. Joining the team were three outstanding rookies also destined for the Hall of Fame: 18-year-old Fred Lindstrom, the youngest player ever to appear in a World Series, barrel-chested Hack Wilson, and "Memphis Bill" Terry. In 1930, Wilson and Terry would set records never equaled: Wilson would slug 56 home runs and drive in a remarkable 190 runs, while Terry would become the last National Leaguer to hit .400.

But 1924 had not been as easy as the previous three seasons for the mighty Giants. Despite their team batting average of .300 for the season, the New Yorkers had barely beaten out the Brooklyn Dodgers, by 1 1/2 games.

The Senators had also been in a fight for the American League pennant. Johnson had started the 1924 season with one more victory than the great Christy Mathewson, and the fans kept expecting Walter to slow down. But through the hot pennant race of August and September, Johnson was magnificent as he racked up win after win. One of those victories was a 2–0 rain-shortened seven-inning no-hitter over the St. Louis Browns on August 25. Three days later,

Opening-game pitchers Walter Johnson (right) and Art Nehf, before taking the mound to start the 1924 World Series. Both veterans went 12 innings, but Nehf won, 4–3, despite 12 strike-outs by Johnson.

the Senators beat the New York Yankees, 11–6, despite two home runs by Babe Ruth, to take over first place from New York. The Yankees stayed close and managed to tie for first place as late as September 18. But the Senators opened up a two-game lead on September 22 when Johnson beat the White Sox, 8–3, for his 13th win in a row. Washington hung on to clinch the pennant in Boston five days later.

Even the most diehard Washington fans figured the Giants would take the Series, but few doubted that Walter Johnson would win at least one game.

Fate had never been kind to Johnson. He had been signed by a last-place team that remained deep in the second division no matter how well he pitched. In the last 9 years, Washington had not even finished second, despite the fact that Johnson usually led the league in victories.

The whole country seemed to be rooting for Johnson when he faced the Giants on the opening day of the Series. His opponent was veteran Art Nehf, a crafty southpaw who specialized in winning World Series games. Nehf had defeated the New York Yankees in each of the past three World Series.

In game 1 of the 1924 Series, Nehf dueled the big, right-handed Johnson for 12 innings and finally triumphed, 4–3. The Giants went on to lose two of the next three games. But after Johnson lost the fifth game, 6–2, the New York-

Fred Lindstrom, the Giants' third baseman, had 4 hits and 2 RBIs to help beat Johnson in game 5 of the 1924 World Series.

ers needed only one more victory to win the world championship.

At Washington's Griffith Stadium on October 9, the Senators' own left-handed star, Tom Zachary, beat Nehf, 2–1, in the sixth game to tie the Series. The final game was to be played the next day. And Walter Johnson, who had pitched a complete game two days earlier, could only watch from the Senator's dugout.

Giants manager John McGraw was a believer in stacking his lineup with right-handed batters when a lefty was pitching and using his left-handed hitters against righties. For the final game, Washington's young player-manager, 27-year-old Bucky Harris, turned the tables on McGraw. Harris started right-handed pitcher Curly Ogden. As Harris had expected, McGraw countered with his left-handed lineup. But Ogden only pitched to the leadoff batter. He was then taken out so that George Mogridge, a lefty who had beaten the Giants in game 4, could come in to face McGraw's left-handed hitters.

The tactic worked perfectly until the 6th inning. But then, with Washington leading, 1–0, the Giants scored three runs and Mogridge was replaced by Fred "Firpo" Marberry. Marberry, one of the first pitchers to make a specialty of being a reliever, did his job.

Neither team scored in the 7th inning, and time was running out for the Senators. They had just two more chances to overcome New York's two-run lead.

In the bottom of the 8th inning, the Senators had runners on second and third with two out when John McGraw called on Art Nehf to relieve starter Virgil Barnes and get the third out. Player-manager Bucky Harris was the batter, and he tapped the ball weakly toward third base. Fred Lindstrom moved to field the ball, but it hit either a clump of dirt or a pebble and bounced over his head. To the Senators' fans, the bad bounce was a miracle. Two runs scored, and the game was tied.

When the Giants came to bat in the 9th inning, there was a new reliever on the mound: Walter Johnson. As the game continued into extra innings, Johnson recalled, "I was in trouble every inning. After getting Fred Lindstrom in the 9th, Frank Frisch hit a fastball to right center for three bases. We decided to pass Ross Youngs, and then I struck out George Kelly and Irish Meusel grounded to third. In the 10th, I walked Hack Wilson and then, after striking out Travis Jackson, I was lucky enough to grab a drive by ol' Hank Gowdy and turn it into a double play. Heinie Groh batted for Hugh McQuillan, the Giant pitcher, in the 11th and singled. Lindstrom bunted him along. I fanned Frisch this time on an outside pitch and once more passed Youngs. Kelly struck out again.

"They kept after me, though. Meusel singled in the 12th, but I'd settled down to believe, by then, that maybe this was my day and I got the next three hitters."

When the Senators came off the field for their turn at bat in the bottom of the 12th inning, Harris told them to bring their gloves with them. At that time, the fielders left their gloves on the field when they changed sides. Harris must have had a feeling that another miracle was in store.

Muddy Ruel, the first batter, lifted a pop foul ball behind home plate. Hank Gowdy, the Giants' veteran catcher, tossed his mask aside, began circling under the ball, then stepped on his mask, stumbled, and dropped the ball. Given another chance, Ruel hit a double. Next, Walter Johnson hit a routine ground ball to the Giants shortstop, Travis Johnson, who booted it away.

While Washington's fans crossed their fingers, Earl McNeeley, the next batter, hit another ground ball. It bounded toward third baseman Fred Lindstrom, and, in what looked like an instant replay of the eighth-inning miracle, the ball hit something on the ground—Lindstrom later called it " the same darned pebble that Harris's ball had hit"—and bounced over the infielder's head. Ruel, a slow runner, chugged around third base. It might have been a close play at the plate, but the Giants left fielder, Irish Meusel, assumed that Lindstrom would make the play and had not moved over to back up third base. By the time Meusel reached the ball, he could do nothing but scoop it up and stick it in his back pocket. Washington had won the world championship— and Walter Johnson finally had a World Series victory after suffering two defeats.

After the game, in the Giants clubhouse, pitcher Jack Bentley expressed his view of the unusual turn of events. "The good Lord," said Bentley, "just couldn't bear to see a fine fellow like Walter Johnson lose again."

Walter Perry Johnson was born on November 6, 1887, near Humbolt, Kansas. When he arrived in the majors, people called the big pitcher with the farmboy complexion and reddish-blond curly hair Swede. Actually, Johnson had a typical early American mixed heritage that traced mostly to the British Isles. Both his parents had Scotch-Irish ancestors, and there was some Dutch and English in the family tree.

Walter's mother, Minnie Olive Perry, had been born on a farm in central Indiana before her family moved to Ohio and then to Kansas. Meanwhile, to escape the poverty of western Pennsylvania, the Johnsons had begun their journey across the midlands of America until they, too, reached Kansas. There the paths of the Perrys and Johnsons met. Young Frank Edwin Johnson and Minnie Olive Perry met at a dance one evening and were married soon after.

Walter Johnson (top row, fifth from left) with his Fullerton (California) High School classmates in 1903.

The newlyweds began their own farm in 1885. It was hard work, but because they were poor, they had no other choice. Minnie Johnson was a strong, wide-shouldered woman. Frank Johnson was not overly tall but he was powerfully built, with broad, sloping shoulders and long arms. His son Walter would have a similar build.

All told, the Johnsons had five children. They all attended the Crescent Valley School in Allen County, near the Oklahoma border. In 1902, when the family moved to Fullerton, California, Walter entered high school. It was there that he played baseball for the first time.

Because Walter was the biggest kid in his class, he started off as the team's catcher. But it soon became clear that he had a lively fastball, and he took up pitching.

His first game was a rout: Walter's team lost 21–0. But it was not the opposing batters who did him in. The problem was that none of his teammates could hold onto his pitches. Johnson would blaze one strike after another across the plate. But on every third strike, the catcher would duck out of the way of the pitch and the batter would reach first safely.

From the first time he threw a baseball, using a natural sidearm motion, Johnson displayed the speed and control that later marked his professional career. As soon as his team got a competent catcher behind the plate, the legend of Walter Johnson began to take shape.

Walter managed to find time for baseball even though he worked after school as a clerk in a feed store. He continued to play after he enrolled at a business college, pitching for Anaheim in a winter league.

One day in 1906, when Johnson pitched against San Diego, a team with some professional players on its roster, he impressed the veterans with his speed and control. One of them, Jack Burnett, an outfielder with the St. Louis Cardinals, talked Walter into going to Tacoma, Washington, to try out for the team in the new Northwestern League.

Walter Johnson's arrival in Tacoma was not the earthshaking event of 1906 on the West Coast—the San Francisco earthquake was. The ballpark where the San Francisco Seals played

In 1907, Idaho State League batters were overmatched against Johnson, the Weiser Wonder. Johnson struck out 211 batters in 135 innings.

Clyde Milan was Walter Johnson's roommate for 15 years with the Washington Senators. The fleet-footed Milan set the A.L. single-season stolen base record in 1912 with 88 thefts. Three years later, Ty Cobb broke the record with 96.

was destroyed, and the team disbanded. Some of the players headed for the new Northwestern League. As a result, there was no place on Tacoma's roster for an untested rookie. Johnson did not make the team. He then heard of a league in Idaho and joined a team in Weiser. He was paid $75 a month, good money for a teenager who was just learning how to play the game. Most of his teammates worked in the mines on weekdays and played ball on weekends. Johnson pitched four games, three of them shutouts, and won all of them.

In 1907, Johnson won the season opener for Weiser, as he would many times for Washington, beating Payette's Melon Eaters, 13–1. Johnson was striking out batters with such regularity that word of his ability traveled all the way up to the majors. His most avid booster was a traveling salesman who bombarded several big-league teams with enthusiastic letters about the young pitcher. William Yawkey, who owned the Detroit Tigers, suggested to his general manager, Frank Navin, that Johnson be scouted. But Navin was not impressed. "If this salesman knows so much about baseball," he scoffed, "what's he doing peddling cigars in bush towns out in Idaho?"

At about this time, another Johnson admirer, a minor-league umpire, touted him to the Pittsburgh Pirates, who were getting ready for the 1907 season. But the Pirates decided not to scout Johnson.

Detroit and Pittsburgh were top teams; they would meet in the 1909 World Series. The Washington Senators were another story altogether. They finished second to last in 1906, and were picked to finish last in 1907. Manager Joe Cantillon was willing to listen to any offer of pitching help.

Cantillon had heard of another youngster, Clyde Milan, a fleet-footed outfielder with a team in Wichita, Kansas. Unfortunately, the Senators were doing so poorly that Cantillon could not afford to send a scout all the way to Kansas to check out a prospect. Then Washington's second-string catcher, Cliff Blankenship, broke a finger and was out of action. While he was recuperating, Cantillon sent him on what turned out to be the most productive scouting expeditions in big-league history. Blankenship first signed Milan for $1,250. "Fleetfoot" Milan would play for 16 seasons in Washington and displace Ty Cobb as the base-stealing champ in 1912 and 1913. But it was Milan's future roommate, Walter Johnson, who was the prize recruit.

Traveling from Kansas, Blankenship reached Idaho on April 28 in time to see Johnson in action. It was a losing effort for Johnson, but the young fireballer, nicknamed The Kid, struck out 17 batters. He won his next game, 3–2, and struck out 13. Finally, Blankenship put a catcher's mitt on and caught the young fireballer. "He knew nothing of the fine points about baseball but he could put more smoke on that old baseball than I had ever dreamed possible," Blankenship later recalled. "I had caught many big-league pitchers but never one with a ball as heavy as the one heaved by Johnson. And with

Joe Cantillon was the first-year manager of the Senators when Walter Johnson was a rookie in 1907. Despite the presence of Johnson, Cantillon's teams won just 35 percent of their games in his three years as manager.

all his speed he had control. He seemed to cut any corner of the plate at will, and more than that I saw he had a head for baseball."

The excited Blankenship would have signed Johnson on the spot, but he had forgotten to bring a contract with him. Undaunted, he led Johnson to the Weiser Butcher Shop, grabbed a piece of brown wrapping paper from the owner, and hurriedly wrote out an agreement for Johnson to sign.

Walter was not quite so eager. First, he wanted to know about travel expenses. "The club will pay for you to come to Washington," Blankenship assured him. "But," asked the cautious Johnson, "will they pay for me to come back to Idaho in case I don't make the team?" He eventually signed the contract only after being guaranteed a round-trip ticket. It was the first of 25 contracts he would sign with Washington—21 as a player and 4 as the team's manager.

Joe Cantillon, whose team would finish last in 1907 despite the presence of Johnson and Milan, was delighted with the success of the scouting mission. "Blankenship was sent up into the woods," he said, "cut down a tall pine and floated it down the creek, and it's a mighty good piece of timber, don't you think?"

3

THE YOUNG PHENOM

Johnson finished the short Idaho State League season with a 14–2 won-lost record, including seven straight shutouts. Among his shutouts were two no-hitters in a row. In one stretch, he pitched 86 consecutive scoreless innings, which would have been an organized-ball record had the league been under the National Agreement. When Johnson departed for Washington, D.C., a host of his friends were at the Weiser train depot to see him off.

It was a tiresome trip for the 19-year-old Walter Johnson. The three day cross-country journey to Washington ended at the Baltimore & Ohio railroad station, where President James Garfield had been assassinated 26 years earlier. Johnson checked into the old Regent, a third-rate hotel, the morning of August 1, 1907, and hustled out to the ballpark to meet his new teammates. Manager Joe Cantillon gave Walter a whole day to rest up from his train trip, then scheduled him to start against the league-leading Detroit Tigers the next day.

"I was the greenest rookie that ever was," Johnson said in an interview many years later.

President William Howard Taft threw out the first ball of the 1910 season and then stayed to watch Johnson throw a one-hitter against the Philadelphia Athletics. The following day, Taft sent a ball to the Washington ace with the inscription: "To Walter Johnson with the hope that he will be as formidable as in yesterday's game."

"One evening I was standing out on the sidewalk when a stranger approached and said, 'You're famous already, kid. See, they've named a hotel after you.' I looked across the street and sure enough, there was a big illuminated sign that read, 'Johnson Hotel.' Well, do you know I was so green that I actually believed that man?"

Johnson was so inexperienced that he walked to the ballpark in his Senators uniform, unaware that he was expected to dress in the clubhouse. Several stories had already appeared in the Washington newspapers about the heralded rookie. Yet less than 500 people showed up to see his debut. Many years later, however, the Washington management invited everyone who had seen Walter Johnson's first game to come as a guest of the team, and 8,000 people claimed the honor.

Sam Crawford, along with Ty Cobb, was a future Hall of Famer who was then in his prime with the Detroit Tigers. Crawford later recalled the newcomer's first game: "Here comes Walter, just a string of a kid, only about 18 or 19 years old. Tall, lanky, from Idaho or somewhere. Didn't even have a curve. Just that fastball. That's all he pitched, just fastballs. He didn't need any curve. We had a terrible time beating him. Late in the game I hit one and it went zooming out over the shortstop's head, and before they could get the ball back in I'd legged it all the way around."

But it was not Crawford's home run that beat Johnson, 3–2; it was a succession of bunted balls started by Ty Cobb. Walter had not yet learned to field his position. He clumsily chased down balls tapped toward third and was slow to cover the base when the ball was fielded by the

*Walter Johnson in 1907,
his rookie year.*

first baseman. The next day, and for weeks afterward, manager Joe Cantillon made Johnson practice fielding bunted balls, helping him become one of the best fielders of all time. In six seasons, he never made an error. There were no Gold Gloves awarded for fielding when Walter Johnson played. But in a time of tiny gloves, he had a career fielding average of .968. Pitcher Jim Kaat, who won 14 Gold Gloves from 1959 to 1983, had a career average of .947. Moreover, Johnson made more assists and putouts than Kaat and committed fewer errors.

No sooner had Johnson learned to field the

bunt than Ty Cobb discovered another way to get at him. The good-natured Johnson's greatest concern was that he would seriously injure a player by hitting him with a pitch. To exploit that fear, Cobb began to crowd the plate. With his toes touching the edge of the plate, he defied Johnson to pitch strikes. Cobb was confident that the gentle pitcher would not brush him back.

Cobb set a style for pesky batters who crowded the plate, choking up on their bats as he did, to poke at Johnson's fastballs. Walter never developed much of a curveball, possibly because of the way batters crowded the plate. He would have had to aim the pitch directly at them. If the pitch failed to break, the risk of injury was too great for Johnson to contemplate.

Still, Johnson could not always avoid hitting batters. He hit a record 206 of them in his career, but none on purpose and only one in the head. Nobody wore helmets in those days.

Only once did Walter Johnson actually try to intimidate a batter. When he was just breaking in, he was persuaded to dust off Frank Baker—

After his 1907 rookie season, Johnson (far left) pitched during the winter for the San Diego Pick-wicks. Future major leaguer Chief Meyers (third from left), a Dartmouth-educated Cahuilla Indian, was Johnson's catcher on the California semi-pro team.

later nicknamed "Home Run" Baker for his World Series slugging—of the Philadelphia Athletics. As the ball whistled under Baker's chin, it was hard to tell who was more frightened: Pitcher and batter were both white-faced. Johnson vowed never again to risk hurting an opponent.

The young pitcher had arrived too late in 1907 to help Washington climb out of last place. The next season, the Senators finished next to last. Johnson managed to break even, with a 14–14 record, in his first full season.

Three of his wins came in four days. All the games were shutouts against the New York Highlanders, who soon became known as the Yankees. Walter blanked the New Yorkers 3–0 on Friday and 6–0 on Saturday. Manager Cantillon knew he had a good thing going, so he asked the obliging youngster to pitch the next game: the first game of a Labor Day doubleheader that Monday. After tossing a two-hit shutout, Johnson then hid until the manager decided to start someone else in the second game. Johnson had injured his arm in the first game, when a line drive struck it. In any event, three consecutive

shutouts in four days was more than the most demanding manager could reasonably expect.

But not even Johnson could do it all by himself. With little support from his teammates, he lost 25 games in 1909 despite posting a 2.21 earned run average. His rookie teammate Bob Groom led the league in losses with 26, while another rookie Senator, Dolly Gray, lost 19.

It was not until 1910 that Johnson finally was able to fashion the kind of record he deserved. He got off to a good start by pitching the season opener. (He would kick off 14 Opening Day games in his long career.) It was during this game that two longstanding baseball traditions began. First, President William Howard Taft, a genuine baseball fan, accepted an invitation to open the new season by throwing out the first ball. Since then, United States presidents have made it a tradition to throw out the season's first pitch.

President Taft also inaugurated a custom that is observed at every major-league game to this day. Weighing close to 300 pounds, he suffered through most of the game because he was uncomfortably wedged into his seat. Finally, after the visitors had batted in the 7th inning, the president squirmed out of his seat and stood up. The fans, seeing the president of the United States standing up, and thinking he was about to depart, also stood up respectfully. But a minute later, Taft resumed his seat and so did the fans. Thus was born the 7th-inning stretch.

Johnson was masterful in the opener against the Philadelphia Athletics, nearly pitching a no-hitter. A fly ball that landed in the crowd that had overflowed onto the field and was ruled a ground-rule double was the only hit for the A's as the

Senators won, 3–0.

Walter Johnson finished the 1910 season with 25 victories. His pitching helped Washington get out of the cellar, although only up one notch, to seventh place. He also won the first of his 12 strikeout titles, fanning 313 batters.

In 1911, Johnson again posted 25 victories. At the end of the season, he bought a farm in Coffeyville, Kansas, for himself and his parents. It would remain his home until he ended his pitching career.

Baseball
Magazine

APRIL

15 Cents

Why I signed with the Federals

J·F·KERNAN

4

THE COMING OF THE OLD FOX

In the April 1915 Baseball Magazine, Johnson explained to baseball fans why he signed with the Federal League's Chicago team. He jumped back to the Washington team, however, and never pitched in the Federal League, which folded after the 1915 season.

Joe Cantillon, the manager who brought Walter Johnson to Washington, was replaced by another veteran of second-division finishes, Jim McAleer, in 1910. But when the Senators remained close to the bottom under his leadership, the owners turned to a man who had already showed he could make a team a winner.

Clark Griffith was to become the most influential person in Walter Johnson's baseball life. A pioneer American League manager, he had led the Chicago White Sox to the league's first pennant in 1901. When the A.L. branched out to New York in 1903, Griffith was put in charge of the Highlanders, and although they did not win a championship, the team finished second twice in its first four years.

As a manager, Griffith was every bit as crafty as he had been when he was pitching for Cap Anson's Chicago White Stockings. Even then he had been called the Old Fox. And throughout his career as a player, manager, and owner, Griffith succeeded by slyly outthinking his opponents.

When Clark Griffith took over in 1912, he jolted new life into the talented but complacent

Washington Senators. There was certainly some talent on the team. Walter Johnson was the best pitcher in baseball. Clyde Milan was a fleet-footed, good-hitting center fielder. At shortstop, the diminutive George McBride was sure-handed. And rookie Chick Gandil was a fine young clean-up batter. In 1912, he batted .305 and drove in 81 runs for Washington.

Given better support and some runs to work with, Johnson won 32 games—16 of them in a row—and the team rose dramatically to second place. Johnson led the league in ERA (1.39) and strikeouts (303).

Walter Johnson's 16 straight wins set an American League record. Earlier in 1912, Rube Marquard, a left-hander with the N.L.'s New York Giants, had won 19 straight. Both pitchers' achievements are still in the record books, although Johnson's 16 has been equaled 3 times.

The Boston Red Sox's ace, Smokey Joe Wood, a year younger than Walter Johnson and considered just as fast, reached 13 in a row late that same season. On September 6, Washington traveled to Boston, and Wood was due to pitch. Johnson would be starting a day ahead of his regular turn in an effort to protect his record from Wood. Fenway Park had just opened that year, and 30,000 fans crowded in for this week-day afternoon game. They jammed the stands and watched the action from behind ropes stretched in back of the outfield and down the foul lines. Years later, Wood recalled, "That was the only game I can remember at Fenway Park, or anywhere else for that matter where the fans were sitting practically along the first-base and third-base lines." The pitching duel was as good as the crowd hoped it would be. Joe Wood finally

won it, 1–0, when the Red Sox scored in the ninth inning. (Washington right fielder Danny Moeller tripped over a spectator sitting on the field and failed to catch a fly ball.) Wood went on to win his next two starts, thereby tying Johnson's mark. His bid to win a 17th straight game was stopped on September 20 when the Detroit Tigers beat him, 6–4 on two unearned runs.

In 1913, the Senators finished second again, six games behind Connie Mack's A's. This time, Johnson won 36 games, with an ERA of 1.09, third lowest of all time. He also led the league in winning percentage (.837), complete games (30), innings pitched (346), and, of course, strikeouts (243). Johnson's individual highlight was pitching 56 consecutive scoreless innings, still an American League record.

It finally appeared that the Washington Senators were hurtling toward an eventual championship, mostly on the strength of Walter Johnson's arm. But when he was not pitching, the Senators won fewer than half their games. As a result, the Philadelphia Athletics held onto first place from May to the season's end. Johnson's spectacular efforts were recognized that October, when he won the Chalmers Award, given to the league's Most Valuable Player.

While Johnson was experiencing his greatest season in 1913, the still painfully shy farm boy was also experiencing his first true romance. He and Clyde Milan now lived at a first-class hotel in Washington, D.C., the Dewey. Among the other residents were the Honorable Edward Roberts, a congressman from Nevada, and his daughter, Hazel. Gazing across the lobby at the young woman, Johnson immediately fell in love with her. However, he was too shy to approach Hazel Lee Roberts, so the couple's first meeting came a while later—at the ball park. Johnson was

Johnson won the Chalmers Award in 1913 as the A.L.'s Most Valuable Player. He had been third in the voting in 1912. As the MVP winner, Johnson (shaking hands with Hugh Chalmer on the left) was awarded a Chalmers '30' automobile.

warming up on the sidelines when he was called over to a nearby box by a man who introduced himself. "I am Representative Roberts," he said. "I've admired you for a long time. You may not know it, but we live in the same hotel."

Of course Johnson knew it. A big grin flashed across his face as Representative Roberts continued: "Mr. Johnson, I would like to present my daughter. Hazel, this is Mr. Johnson."

The courtship was almost as rapid as Walter's fastball, and the bashful young pitcher soon blurted out a proposal. Hazel Roberts accepted, and they were married before the season ended. It was a storybook romance, just made to order for Washington. The capital's greatest athlete had married the daughter of a congressman. As soon as the baseball season ended, Walter and Hazel traveled to Coffeyville, where they made their home on the Johnson farm. In the years that followed, they had five children: Walter, Jr.; Eddie; Bob; Carolyn Anne; and Barbara Joan.

As his family responsibilities steadily increased, Walter Johnson could no longer afford to accept whatever salary was offered to him by the Senators. And he now had a choice. In 1914, a third major league, the Federal League, came into existence and began to hire players away from the National and American leagues. The Federal League survived its first season and again went after the top stars of the established leagues for the 1915 season. They promised Walter Johnson $25,000 a year for three seasons. That amount sounded pretty good to Johnson, who had been offered just $12,500 a year by Benjamin Minor, president of the Washington club. The Senators had slipped back to third place, and Minor had suggested that some of the blame could be attributed to the fact that Walter had won only 28 games.

Having just led the league in victories again, pitched the most innings (372), been in the most games (51), thrown the most shutouts (9), and once again topped the strikeout leaders (225), Johnson had asked for a boost to $16,000, with a $6,000 bonus for signing for 3 years. Walter might have been shy around girls, but he was not bashful about asking for what he thought he was worth. And the letter from Washington, which threatened to hold him to his old salary of $10,000 if he did not accept the Senators' offer of $12,500, made even the mild-mannered Johnson angry.

The Federal League sent Joe Tinker, the manager of the new league's Chicago team, to Coffeyville with an offer. Johnson had already talked to the league during the summer, and now, fueled by his anger at Minor, he accepted Tinker's offer, pocketing a $7,500 bonus for signing.

The news that Walter Johnson had joined the upstart Federal League sent Washington manager Clark Griffith rushing to Kansas. The loyal Walter Johnson was caught in a bind when the Old Fox predicted that his defection would ruin the franchise. Griffith explained he was raising the capital to buy out Minor, but without Walter Johnson on the team there was no way he could get the backing to take over.

There still remained the matter of the cash bonus Walter Johnson had accepted. Even if the Senators could scrape up enough money to match Johnson's new salary, they could not replace the $7,500 he had already received from Chicago. Or could they? The Old Fox certainly thought so. He went straight to Chicago and talked to Charles Comiskey, owner of the American League's Chicago White Sox. Comiskey, whose tightness with players' salaries, eventually tempted eight of them to throw the 1919 World Series, was a practical man. He handed Griffith $7,500 after the Old Fox asked, "How many customers do you think you'll lose on days when Walter Johnson is across town pitching for the Feds?" And with that, the Federal League's bonus was repaid. Walter Johnson remained with Washington for the rest of his career.

Season of 1925
Clark Griffith Stadium
Opening Game April 22, 1925.

Mgr Huggins
New York

Mgr Harris
Washington

Pres. Coolidge
throwing out the first ball
Left to right - Sec. Treas. Mellon
Mrs Coolidge - President Coolidge - Sec. State Kellogg

Sec. of State Kellogg raising the Flag

Judge   Harris   Johnson   watching
the "Goose" knocking 'em over the fence in practice

5

THE BIG TRAIN STEAMS ALONG

It was Grantland Rice, the dean of American sportswriters, who named Walter Johnson the Big Train. "The 'Big Train' is coming to town," Rice wrote in his syndicated column, and people knew the reliable Walter Johnson was on track.

Ballplayers and friends, however, had another nickname for him. Barney Oldfield was the nation's fastest racing car driver, and when Walter Johnson was awarded a Chalmers automobile as the American League's Most Valuable Player in 1913, he began to drive around Washington at then breakneck speeds of up to 25 miles per hour. That was enough to earn him the nickname Barney.

In 1915, Walter Johnson continued to be the Senators' top pitcher. But Clark Griffith could not keep the team anywhere near first place. For the next 5 years, Johnson posted 20 or more wins each season. In three of those years, he led the league in victories. He would pitch the season opener,—more often than not a shutout— add a ball autographed by the president to the collection he later donated to the Baseball Hall of Fame, and add another line or two to the

The scenes from the opening day of the 1925 season show a variety of pre-game activities. Johnson (lower left photo, far right) and teammates Joe Judge and Bucky Harris watch batting practice.

Johnson was a solid hitter who occasionally played the outfield and pinchhit. In 1925, he hit .433, the highest batting average ever compiled by a pitcher.

record books.

Year after year, Johnson led the league in strikeouts. But then, in 1920, he developed a sore arm. The spring-training weather had been miserable, and Johnson caught a severe cold. The pain settled into his arm and lingered there. That year, he missed Opening Day, and it took him months to find his form.

Then, on July 1, 1920, he hurled the only no-hitter of his career. It took one of those miracles that so often worked in Johnson's favor to save his no-hit bid against the Boston Red Sox. With two out in the ninth inning, Red Sox player-manager Harry Hooper slashed a sizzling drive that seemed sure to fly by first baseman Joe Judge. But Judge made a spectacular dive, knocked the ball down, and threw to Johnson, who was covering first base. The no-hitter was saved. It was fitting that the first no-hitter in Washington Senators' history was thrown by their star, Walter Johnson. Johnson was also pleased because the no-hitter came on his son's fifth birthday.

But apart from that great moment, it seemed as if the decade of averaging more than 300 innings a year had taken its toll. For the first time in 10 years, he lost more than he won, finishing the season with a 8–10 record. The Senators wound up in sixth place.

Clark Griffith, who had slowly accumulated enough stock in the team to become the majority owner, gave up managing and became president of the team. In 1921, the Senators got a new manager, George McBride, and a new name for their remodeled park, Griffith Stadium.

Johnson was past his peak when the 1920s began, but he was still able to keep his strikeout title in 1921, 1923, and 1924. He no longer could pitch more than 300 innings. Yet as it turned out, the aging pitcher, now in his late thirties, was getting ready for one final assault on the goal that had so long eluded him—a World Series victory.

In 1924, Clark Griffith showed just how foxy he could be: He replaced manager George McBride with second baseman Bucky Harris. Called the Boy Manager, the 27-year-old Harris turned out to be an inspired choice.

Johnson got the team off to its annual good start with another Opening Day shutout. On May 23, he struck out 14 White Sox batters in a 4–0, one-hit victory, his fourth shutout of the young season.

With Johnson regaining his old form, the

Senators fought the New York Yankees all the way for the American League championship. Washington clinched it just two days before the season ended. Babe Ruth had led New York to successive pennants in 1921, 1922, and 1923. But even though Ruth had a great season in 1924, winning his only batting title, with a .378 average, and topping the league in home runs, Walter Johnson had an even better one. He was voted the American League's Most Valuable Player for 1924.

Never missing a turn on the mound, Johnson led the league in wins with 23, in ERA with 2.72, in winning percentage with .767, in shutouts with 6, and, of course, in strikeouts with 158. This was a low total compared to his youthful days, when he had topped 300 each season, but better than anyone else could do.

The 1924 World Series provided a roller-coaster ride for the emotions of America's baseball fans. Because of Walter Johnson, Washington was the sentimental favorite. John McGraw's New York Giants were playing their fourth World Series in a row and were loaded with superstars, so it would not be easy for Johnson to manage to get his first World Series win. But, in the 13th inning of the seventh game, he nailed down his team's first world championship.

With a World Series ring on his finger, the 37-year-old Johnson considered hanging up his glove. His Kansas farm was prospering, and he had a wonderful marriage with five fine children. Actually, he had thought of retiring to a quiet life in Coffeyville several years earlier. Only the pleas of Clark Griffith and his own determination to play for a championship team and win a World Series game had kept him going for so long.

But Johnson was still not ready to retire. Having enjoyed one of his best seasons ever in 1924, he was back on the mound in 1925. He was not quite as good as the year before. Although he won 20 games, he was not even the leading pitcher on the staff. Veteran spitballer Stan Coveleski also won 20 games but lost only 5, compared to Johnson's 7. The two pitchers finished first and second in the league in winning percentage. Where Johnson surprisingly took up the slack was at the plate. Always a dependable batter, he hit an incredible .433, the best average ever for a pitcher, in 95 at bats. As a pinch-hitter, he even belted out a pair of home runs. And he was perfect as ever with his glove, fielding 1.000.

The 1925 pennant came easier than the year before. With an ailing Babe Ruth missing a third

After the U.S. entered World War I in 1917, many major leaguers joined the armed forces. In a pre-game march to show their support in 1918, the Washington team was led by Franklin D. Roosevelt, the assistant secretary of the Navy, and later president of the United States.

of the Yankees' games, the New Yorkers plunged to seventh place. The Philadelphia Athletics challenged Washington but finished $8\frac{1}{2}$ games out of first at season's end. It looked as if the World Series—this one against the Pittsburgh Pirates—would be easier to win, too. Even though Johnson twisted his leg just before the Series began and pitched the first game with his thigh heavily wrapped, he breezed through to a 4–1 victory.

Pittsburgh's Vic Aldrich evened the series the next day, outpitching Coveleski, 3–2. Washington regained the lead, however, when Alex Ferguson, a surprise starter who had been with three teams in 1925, won another close game, 4–3. In game 4, back-to-back homers by Goose Goslin and Joe Harris in the 3rd inning staked Johnson to a four-run lead, and he scattered six hits in a 4–0 shutout. The win left the Senators up three games to one, and it seemed to be all over but the shouting. Even if Washington lost the next two and let Pittsburgh tie the series, Johnson would be available to pitch the final game.

The year before, one might have thought that the fates had planned the bounce of every ball in the final game simply so Walter Johnson could win. But in 1925, it looked more as if demons were conspiring to bring about his downfall. Aldrich again stopped the Senators in the fifth game, 6–3, and the next day, back in Pittsburgh, Remy Kremer outdueled Ferguson, 3–2. Joe Harris almost tied the game up for Washington in the 9th inning, but his bid for a homer bounced off a screen in center field that had been put up for the World Series. He settled for a double and was left stranded on base. Now the teams were all tied up with three wins apiece.

Judge Kenesaw Mountain Landis became commissioner of baseball in 1921 and ruled the sport with an iron fist until his death in 1944.

That night, a drenching rainstorm hit the eastern seaboard, and the all-important seventh game was canceled by Commissioner Judge Landis. It was still raining when Thursday, October 15, dawned. A tarpaulin had been spread across the diamond, but the outfield at Forbes Field was almost a swamp. Still, 42,856 fans, most of them carrying umbrellas, streamed through the turnstiles.

Judge Landis sat unhappily in his box seat beside the field, with water dripping off the brim of his soggy fedora. Landis was in a quandary. Only in his second year as commissioner, he was undecided whether to delay the game or not. Reluctantly, he allowed the game to begin.

The tarp was removed and the ground crew began bringing sawdust to help dry up the area around home plate. During the game, there were

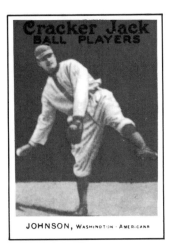

*Walter Johnson's 1914
Cracker Jack card.*

repeated trips to the batter's box with wheelbarrows full of sawdust. No one seemed to care, though, that the pitcher's mound was turning into a mud hill. All Walter Johnson could do was fill his cap with some sawdust and sprinkle it around the mound in a vain attempt to improve his footing.

Despite the difficult conditions, the game started favorably for Johnson, with the Senators scoring four runs in the 1st inning. By the end of the 4th, they led, 6–3. However, Johnson was finding it increasingly difficult to grip the slippery ball and keep his balance during his follow-through. Shortstop Roger Peckinpaugh, who had succeeded Walter Johnson as the American League's MVP, was having troubles of his own. He had already made six errors in the first six games. Today, he would boot two more. The muddy infield looked like chocolate pudding as balls skidded through the slop.

Once the game was under way, Judge Landis hesitated to bring it to a halt. If he had stopped the game after the 5th or 6th inning, Washington, ahead by two runs, would have won the game. When the Pirates tied the game in the bottom of the 7th, it would have been merciful to stop. But Landis refused to do so.

The Pirates came to bat in the bottom of the 8th, and the rain got worse. Wisps of fog hung over the outfield. There were two men out and two on base when Kiki Cuyler, the Pirates' best batter, wiped the rain out of his eyes and looked out at the mound. The count went to 2 and 2, and then Johnson found enough footing to whip a fastball across the heart of the plate. The rain must have blurred the umpire's vision, because he called it a ball. Cuyler drove the next pitch deep into the right-field corner, and two runs came in to score. All the umpires were stationed in the infield, which was the practice at the time, and it was all but impossible to see a ball hit to the outfield. Years later, Goose Goslin remembered the ball: "The umpires couldn't see it. It was too dark and foggy. It wasn't fair at all. It was foul by two feet. I know because the ball hit in the mud and *stuck* there." The Senators raged that the ball was foul, but the umpire's decision stood. Washington went out numbly in the 9th inning, and the final score was 9–7, Pittsburgh.

In the 1924 Series, the Big Train had lost his first two starts and then had dramatically won the seventh game. This time, he had easily won the first two games and had been derailed in the final game. It looked like the end of the line for Walter Johnson.